SCIENCE IN OUR WORLD

PATTERNS
and
SHAPES

Contributory Author
Brian Knapp, BSc, PhD
Art Director
Duncan McCrae, BSc
Special models
*Tim Fulford, MA, Head of Design and Technology,
Leighton Park School*
Special photography
Graham Servante
Editorial consultant
Rita Owen
Illustrations
David Woodroffe
Science advisor
*Jack Brettle, BSc, PhD, Chief Research Scientist,
Pilkington plc*
Print consultants
Landmark Production Consultants Ltd
Printed and bound in Hong Kong
Produced by
EARTHSCAPE EDITIONS

First published in the United Kingdom in 1992
by Atlantic Europe Publishing Company Limited,
86 Peppard Road, Sonning Common, Reading,
Berkshire, RG4 9RP, UK

Publication Data

Knapp, Brian
    Patterns and shapes – (Science in our world; 21)
    1. Pattern perception – For children
    2. Form perception – For children
    I. Title   II. Series
516.15

ISBN 1-869860-81-0

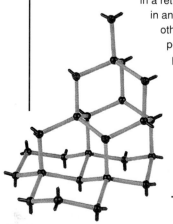

In this book you will find some words that have been shown in **bold** type. There is a full explanation of each of these words on pages 46 and 47.

On many pages you will find experiments that you might like to try for yourself. They have been put in a yellow box like this.

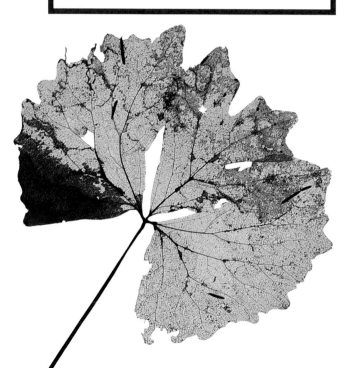

Acknowledgements
The publishers would like to thank the following:
Dr Angus McCrae, Micklands County Primary
School, Nigel Phillips, Redlands County Primary
School, and The Goldfish Bowl.

Picture credits
t=top b=bottom l=left r=right

All photographs from the Earthscape Editions
photographic library except the following:
Keith Wheeler 40/41, 41b, 44/45;
NASA 18, 21tr; ZEFA 37.

Contents

Introduction

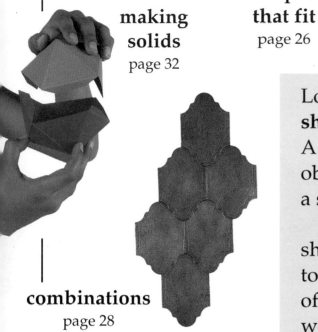

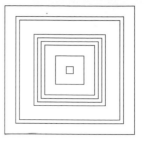

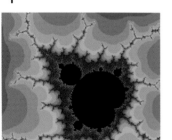

Look at your left hand, it has a definite **shape** which is easily recognised. A shape describes the outline of any object. It can be your hand, a glass, a skyscraper or the Earth.

Most things have very complicated shapes and they can be quite difficult to describe. Try describing the shape of your hand without using common words like finger, thumb or palm and you will quickly see how difficult even familiar objects are to describe.

Look more closely at the ends of your fingers and see the ridges on the surface of your skin that help to give you grip. There are many similar ridges which – as a group – make a **pattern**.

In this book you will find that simple patterns can make up even the most complicated shapes.

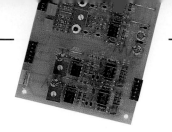

Patterns of simple shapes are important in our world. For example, bricks are arranged in a pattern to make a wall and stitches are made into patterns during sewing. When people invent patterns they are called **designs** and some of them can be used for decoration.

Patterns allow us to build large shapes from small ones. The building blocks of everything in the **Universe** are the small shapes of **atoms**.

People have studied patterns and shapes for thousands of years and they form part of a study called geometry. Find out about the exciting world of patterns and shapes. Just turn to a page to begin your discoveries.

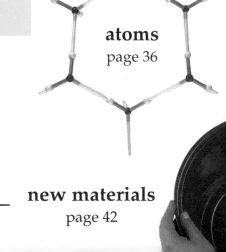

Dots and dashes

The simplest marks on a piece of paper are dots and dashes. But these two tiny marks can be made into shapes and patterns that allow blind people to read or for anyone to keep in touch across the world.

Dots

A dot is a small round mark on a paper and because it is so simple it is easily made time after time by very simple machines.

A pattern of dots can also give a surprising amount of information. Sixty three patterns of dots can be made from just two rows of three dots. This is more than enough to allow each letter of the alphabet to have its own unique dot pattern.

Dots give the numbers for games like dominoes. This enabled dominoes to be played by people who cannot read

Patterns of dots on dice provide many combinations of numbers

This is the pattern of six dots in two columns that Louis Braille used to make his system to enable the blind to 'read'

Using bumps for dots

A pattern of dots can be used in many ways. Braille got his idea for a system of bumps for dots from the method the French army used for passing messages at night during a battle. Try finding ways of making a message using Braille-type bumps, holes or dips. Which is easiest for the fingers to recognise?

```
• — — — —    (1)
• • — — —    (2)
• • • — —    (3)
• • • • —    (4)
• • • • •    (5)
— • • • •    (6)
— — • • •    (7)
— — — • •    (8)
— — — — •    (9)
— — — — —   (10)
```

The Morse Code

One way to send information is to switch the electricity supply on and off in a pattern. This produces a set of clicks – the electrical version of dots. This is how the telegraph works.

In early telegraphs an operator would tap in the code at one end and another operator would listen to the pattern of clicks at the other end.

To make the pattern easy to understand and remember, Morse used long and short clicks (called dots and dashes) for his pattern. In this way he produced the Morse Code.

The Braille system is made by pressing into the paper to make a pattern of bumps on the other side. It is called embossing.

A pattern of bumps is more easily felt by the fingers than, for example, a pattern of holes punched into the paper

A (1)	B (2)	C (3)	D (4)	E (5)	F (6)	G (7)	H (8)	I (9)

J (0)	K	L	M	N	O	P	Q	R

S	T	U	V	W	X	Y	Z

Patterns that mean yes or no

Dots and dashes, or 0s and 1s can be used to make messages when combined in a particular way. They can also be used to add up and even to give instructions to machines. Although they seem such simple instructions, and they have been in use for thousands of years, they form the basis of even the most powerful **computers**.

You will find a bar code on the back of this book and on many other things that you buy. The bar code is a set of thick and thin bars, each spaced across a strip. By reading the pattern of lines, their width and the spaces between them, special light beam readers can identify the book

A series of light emitting **diodes** (called LEDs) or a **laser** beam shine a red light onto the bar code. Next to each LED there is a light-sensitive cell. When the beam shines on a black bar no light is reflected and the cell does not switch on (instruction: yes, there is a bar at this position); where there is white space light reaches the cell and it sends the instruction: no, there is no bar at this position. This allows a computer to read the number on the bar code

ISBN 1-869860-81-0

9 781869 860813

The abacus is a system of beads which represent numbers. They are like dots on the paper.

Beads are moved up and down the pins to do all the normal types of arithmetic. It is a simple form of calculator

Computers and the binary system

A computer is a very fast machine that uses a very simple arithmetic system – it can only understand patterns of yes or no. In the case of a computer it reads 1 (one) or 0 (zero). The system of making everything out of patterns of 1s and 0s is called the **binary system**. Here are some numbers made into the binary system.

How patterns make numbers
The simple rule of one and zero (dot and dash) arithmetic are

$$0 \qquad 0 \qquad 1$$
$$+0 \qquad +1 \qquad +1$$
$$=0 \qquad =1 \qquad =10$$

So '2' is 10 in the binary system as shown in the table.

Decimal		Binary			
Place 10	Place 1	Place 8	Place 4	Place 2	Place 1
	0				0
	1				1
	2			1	0
	3			1	1
	4		1	0	0
	5		1	0	1
	6		1	1	0
	7		1	1	1
	8	1	0	0	0
	9	1	0	0	1
1	0	1	0	1	0

(For more information on computers see the book Computers and Robots *in the Science in our World series.)*

Fingerprints

There are many patterns on the skin of your hands. There are patterns of creases which make it easier to move your hand and there are patterns on each fingertip which give grip. But even such simple patterns can be **unique**.

Everyone to their own

Every fingerprint is unique and yet it can be classified into one of three basic patterns – arches, loops and whorls. Each basic pattern can be subdivided to make eight types and these types further subdivided by counting ridges.

A double loop type

A plain arch type

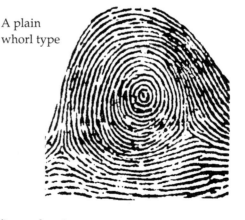

A plain whorl type

A finger showing a central pocket loop type of ridge pattern

Find out about your hand patterns
To study your fingerprints you will need an ink pad and some white paper. Press your fingertip down onto the pad and then press your finger onto the paper.

Compare the pattern of lines on your fingerprint with those shown on this page to find out what type of ridge pattern you have. Then compare your ridge pattern with those of your friends and see how many points of difference you can find.

The police use fingerprint patterns to help identify the people who have committed crimes. You may be able to ask your local police station to show you how this is done.

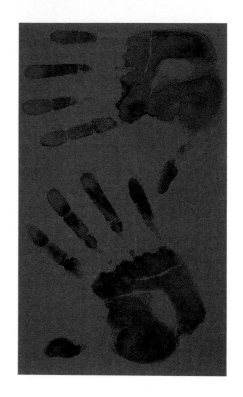

A radial loop type

A central pocket loop type

An accidental type

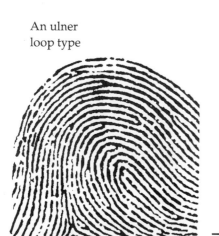

An ulner loop type

A tented arch type

Routes

If you make a journey you are following a route. A route is a line between two points, a simple kind of geometric pattern.

Many people – such as those making deliveries – want to find the shortest route because it saves them time and fuel costs. However, finding the shortest route is often not at all easy.

Route finder

Suppose you want to make a delivery to each home on the blocks shown in the diagram below? What is the shortest route you can find?

Try it for yourself by making a tracing of the diagram and mark a route in pencil. Lay a piece of cotton over the pencil line you have drawn and then compare the cotton line lengths with those of your friends.

Do you think you could find a shorter path if the blocks were differently shaped? Try out any idea you may have.

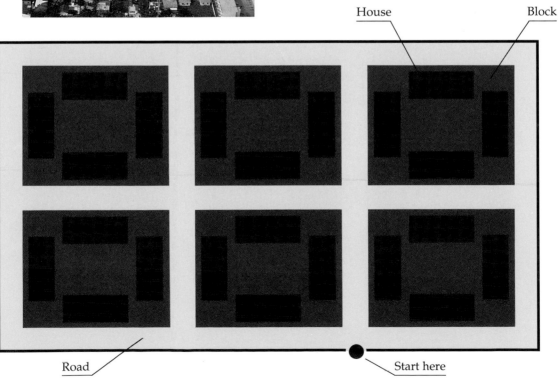

House   Block

Road   Start here

12

Making routes easier to follow

Many routes are very complicated and hard to follow. Think of the journey from your home to school. If you were trying to tell someone how to get to your school would you be most concerned with distances, or with easily recognised 'route flags' such as road junctions and traffic signals?

It is common to find route maps redrawn with changed shapes. This is shown in the pictures on this page. Which do you find easiest to follow?

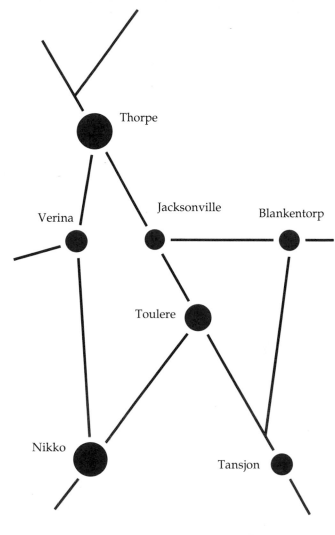

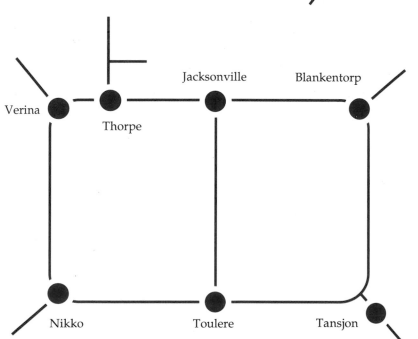

Finding your way across a network
Find a bus, train or underground railway map and compare the shape of the network with the real routes and locations of stops and termini. Does the network map show true distances or shapes or does it look more like the drawing on the left?

Never-ending lines

The Mobius strip is one of the strangest shapes you will find and it also has some exciting properties. You can think of it as a route with no ending.

Make a Mobius strip

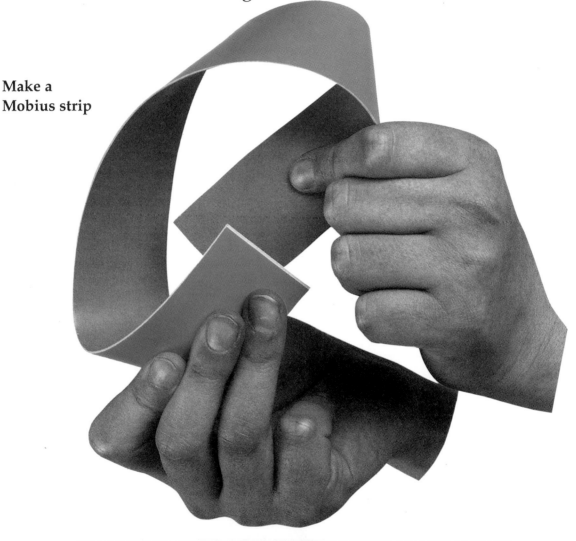

Start with a strip of paper, preferably with a different colour on each side. Any size strip can be used but a good starting size would be 50 cm long and about 5 cm wide.

Pick up the strip and twist one end over, then bring the ends together and gum them to make a twisted band.

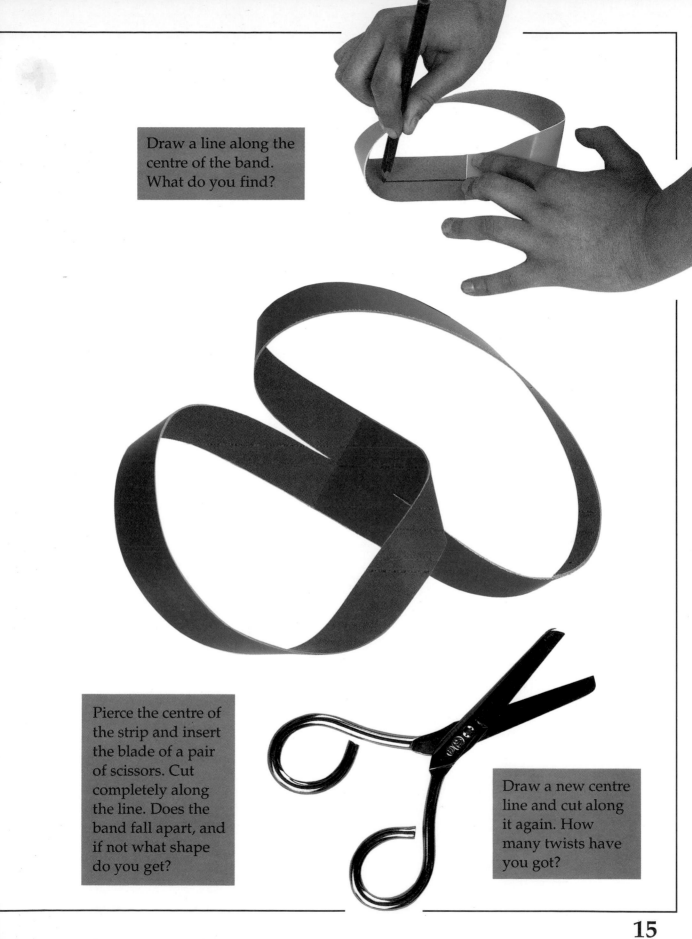

Draw a line along the centre of the band. What do you find?

Pierce the centre of the strip and insert the blade of a pair of scissors. Cut completely along the line. Does the band fall apart, and if not what shape do you get?

Draw a new centre line and cut along it again. How many twists have you got?

Circuit diagrams

A printed circuit is composed of a set of wires connecting various **components** together. In a circuit it is vitally important that the right connections are made, but usually it doesn't much matter what the pattern of the linking wires looks like.

The printed circuit is an important example of *designing* a pattern with the wires to make the links easy to follow even on a complicated piece of equipment such as a computer.

Even your telephone and your wrist watch have printed circuit boards inside them

This is the back of the printed circuit board shown on the opposite page. The wires are strips of metal that are fixed on to the board to make them less likely to break.

The pattern is designed to make sure that each component is linked without wires crossing over one another.

Try following the wires to see which components they connect

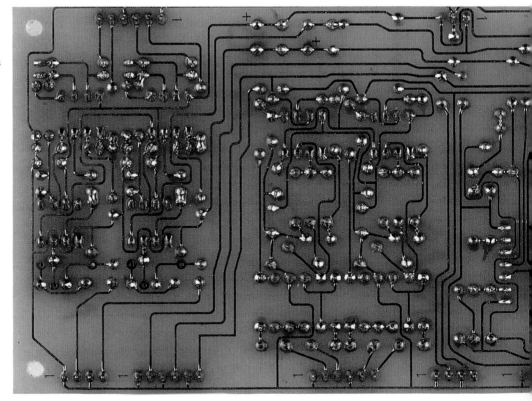

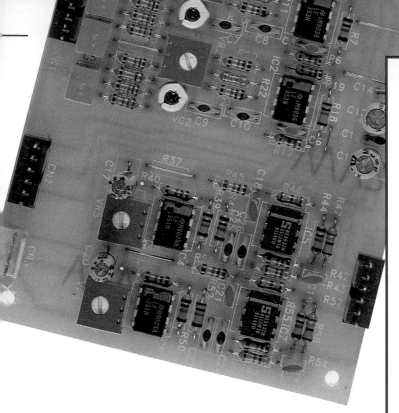

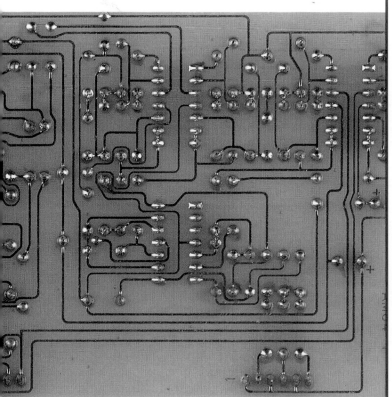

This is part of the front of a printed circuit board. You can just see the wires through the board. Notice how the components have been designed to fit the board

Designing a printed circuit

You can try to design a printed circuit board that will connect five pegs in a pegboard sheet with five elastic bands.

Set out a pegboard as shown in the upper picture. Pull each band in such a way that it will still be attached to the same pegs but will no longer cross any other band. One step has been done for you in the lower picture. You can see that the way to do it is to use additional pegs.

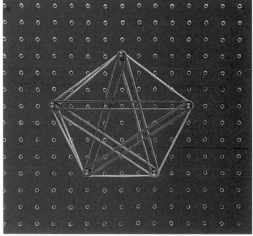

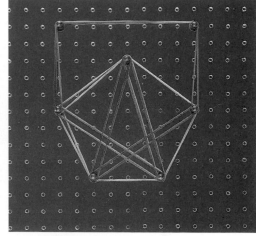

Branching

Branching is a pattern of dividing or combining. It occurs commonly in nature (such as in the blood vessels in our bodies, the veins in a leaf, or the **tributaries** of a river). It is also used for providing electricity and water to our homes and taking waste water away for disposal.

This is a pattern of branching rivers. Rivers gather water from the land, sending it to a trunk stream that eventually leads to the sea

?	
?	
21	(8+13)
13	(5+8)
8	(3+5)
5	(2+3)
3	(1+2)
2	**branches**
1	**trunk**

Electrical branches
Branching can be seen on the fuse board of your home. A single thick cable comes to your home from the street supply. It is then routed to the wall sockets, the light fitting and cooker, heating and shower units through a fuse board. A similar fuse board and branching pattern occurs in all homes.

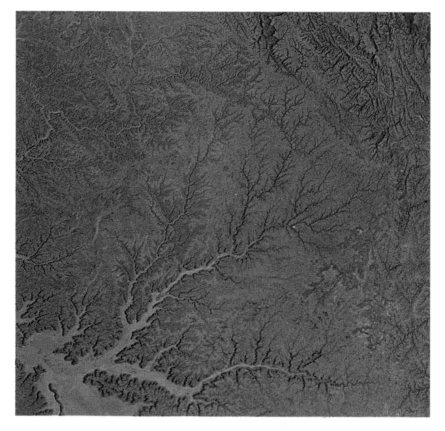

Leaves that have partly rotted often show the pattern of veins very clearly. You can find such leaves in a woodland, park, garden or even beneath a houseplant

Leaf

Despite differences in *shape*, many natural things share the same basic pattern.

A leaf, for example, has branching ribs spread evenly over the surface, with large ribs connecting with smaller ones.

Follow a rib from the leaf edge by making a tracing of the leaf on this page. When you come to a branch, trace the branch as well.

Repeat the tracing for a leaf you have picked up for yourself. When you have done this for both leaves look at the kind of branching you have traced. Are they similar? If they are it suggests that branching is very important pattern for a plant.

Spirals

Our world has many examples of curved lines. Many are regular curves such as circles, but some curves make particularly beautiful shapes called spirals. There are many kinds of spiral; some of which are shown on this page.

Look at the scales on a pineapple (below) or a pine cone (above). They are set in the form of a spiral

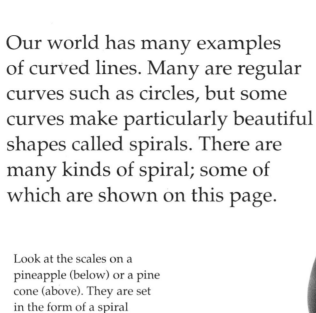

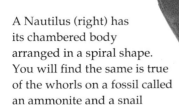

A Nautilus (right) has its chambered body arranged in a spiral shape. You will find the same is true of the whorls on a fossil called an ammonite and a snail

An Archimedian spiral

One common type of spiral was discovered by the Greek scientist Archimedes and it can be made using a record player, two pieces of card, an empty cotton reel and a pencil. (Ask a grown-up to help you with this because you must take care of the playing arm and pick-up).

Cut a disc from stiff card the same size as a record player turntable. Make a hole in the centre and fit it over the turntable. Cut a rectangle of card like the one shown in the picture below. The slot should be wide enough for a cotton reel to slide up and down inside.

Fit the pencil in the cotton reel and switch the player on to manual. (In this position the arm will not swing out). Hold the free end of the rectangular card and, while the turntable is rotating, boldly draw the pencil evenly from one end of the slot to the other. You will see a curve appear on the rotating card. By changing the speed you move the pencil along the slot you can draw a number of spirals.

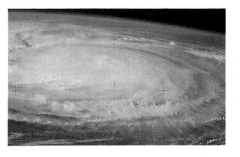

As the wind moves towards the centre of a tropical storm it is spun round. The resulting spiralling pattern of cloud is very like the pattern you get in the experiment below

Cardboard with slot cut out. Hold this end

Pencil inside a cotton reel. Move the pencil along the slot evenly

Cardboard disc placed on record turntable set to manual

Chaos

The Mandelbrot set
This is a group, or set, of patterns that appear the same no matter what scale you look at them. They are named after the mathematician who first described them.

Mandelbrot and similar sets suggest that it is possible for very complicated patterns and shapes to be made from very simple rules. This may even help us to understand more clearly how each different living thing is able to form from simple instructions within cells (see also page 44).

There are many very complicated patterns that are hard to predict and seem **chaotic** in nature but they all obey certain simple rules. The way the clouds form and move across the sky, or the way wisps of steam rise from a hot cup of coffee are apparently made by **random** movements of spiralling air.

The patterns on these page appear very complicated, but they are produced from very simple **formulae** that are calculated many millions of times by a computer. As the computer calculates, so it draws shapes, called fractals, which it fills in with colour. However, even tiny changes in the formula will lead to spectacular differences between one pattern and the next.

Make chaos patterns
Personal computers are now powerful enough to be able to make these patterns. Ask a grown-up to look out a 'chaos' software program and then run it on a personal computer to make patterns of your own.

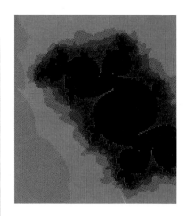

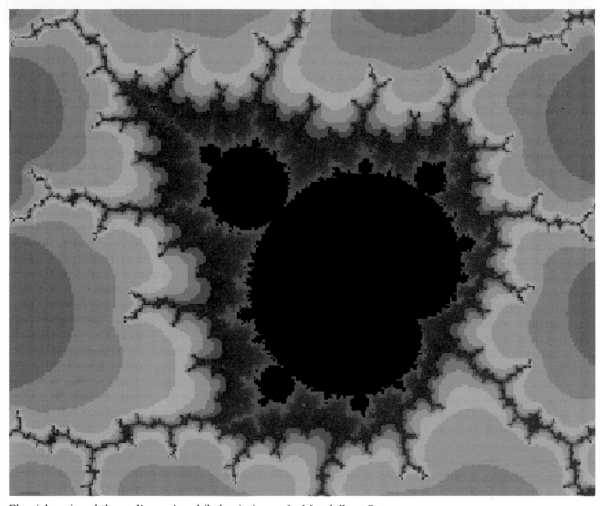

Plan (above) and three-dimensional (below) views of a Mandelbrot Set

Squares and rectangles

Squares are four-sided shapes where all the sides are of equal length and all the corners at right angles. Rectangles are 'stretched' squares, with one pair of sides longer than the other.

Squares and rectangles are used in many everyday situations, but patterns of squares and rectangles can be more difficult to fit together than you might think.

Squares inside squares
Make a tracing of the chess board below. Notice that there are 64 small squares. Using combinations of small squares, try to see how many larger squares can be fitted on to the table. Try, for example, groups of four small squares. Can you fit more squares when they are of many different sizes?

A square has four equal sides

The squares on this chess board fit together to cover the playing surface of the board

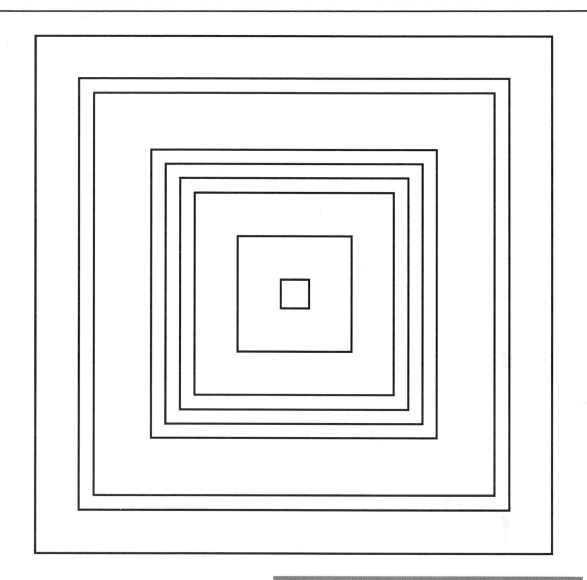

Dividing squares

The diagram above shows nine squares that have been drawn one inside the other. Trace each square onto a separate piece of paper and then cut them out. Try to rearrange them to make one large square.

Giant metal containers are used to carry many types of goods. They are really huge three dimensional rectangles. It is particularly helpful if the goods that go inside the container are packed in boxes made of standard sizes that will fill it completely

Fitting shapes together

Many shapes are regular, that is their sides have equal lengths. Many regular shapes fit together and cover a surface, but only when they have fewer than seven sides. Some irregular shapes will also fit together as we shall see on the next page.

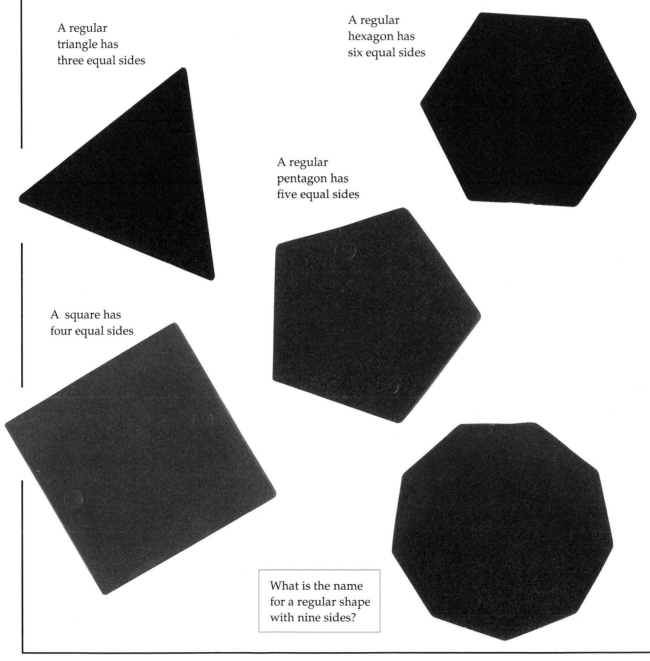

A regular triangle has three equal sides

A regular hexagon has six equal sides

A regular pentagon has five equal sides

A square has four equal sides

What is the name for a regular shape with nine sides?

A regular octagon has eight equal sides

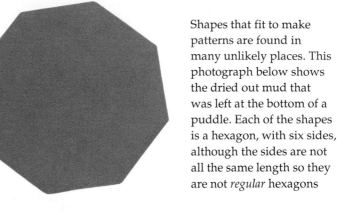

Shapes that fit to make patterns are found in many unlikely places. This photograph below shows the dried out mud that was left at the bottom of a puddle. Each of the shapes is a hexagon, with six sides, although the sides are not all the same length so they are not *regular* hexagons

A regular septagon has seven sides

Which shapes fit together?
Some regular shapes fit together to exactly leaving no spaces. When they do this they make a pattern called a **tessellation**. Using coloured card, cut out six copies of each of the shapes on the opposite page and find out which shapes fit together perfectly.

Then try to find mixtures of these shapes. (Hint: You may need to cut new, smaller, squares to help fill in some of the holes.)

Can you see which shapes fit together to make the surface of a football?

Combining patterns

Not all shapes used to cover a surface have to be so obviously regular as those in the previous page. For example, if you look at a piece of patterned wallpaper it may not at first appear to have any regular pattern. But even the most complicated patterns still have to obey certain rules.

Wallpaper puzzle
Wallpaper is made in long rolls, but when it is hung on to a wall it must appear to give a pattern. Using a roll of wallpaper investigate how designers make this happen and how much 'wastage' is created.

Tiles are simple shapes that make patterns to cover floors, walls and ceilings. But even the most fancy tiles are based on interlocking shapes where the shape on one side matches the shape on the other. They are really mirror images of each other

Design
The design on the page opposite makes a pattern which could be used on fabrics. Look at it carefully and decide which shapes make up the pattern. Then try making a design from other combinations of the shapes on page 26.

Solid shapes

The patterns on the previous page have only two **dimensions**, and they lie flat on a sheet of paper. Most objects are in three dimensions, that is they are solid shapes.

These are also the building blocks for many familiar shapes in our world.

A solid cylinder has a circular cross-section. Example: needle

A crystal of copper sulphate has a shape based on a **parallelogram** and a rectangle

A solid pentagonal **prism** has a five-sided cross-section. This is not common in nature because five-sided solids do not stack together well

Solid examples
Examples of some solid shapes are given on these pages. Find out and list examples of the others.

A pyramid with a square base. Example: fence post top

A hexagonal prism has a cross-section that is a hexagon. Example: pencil

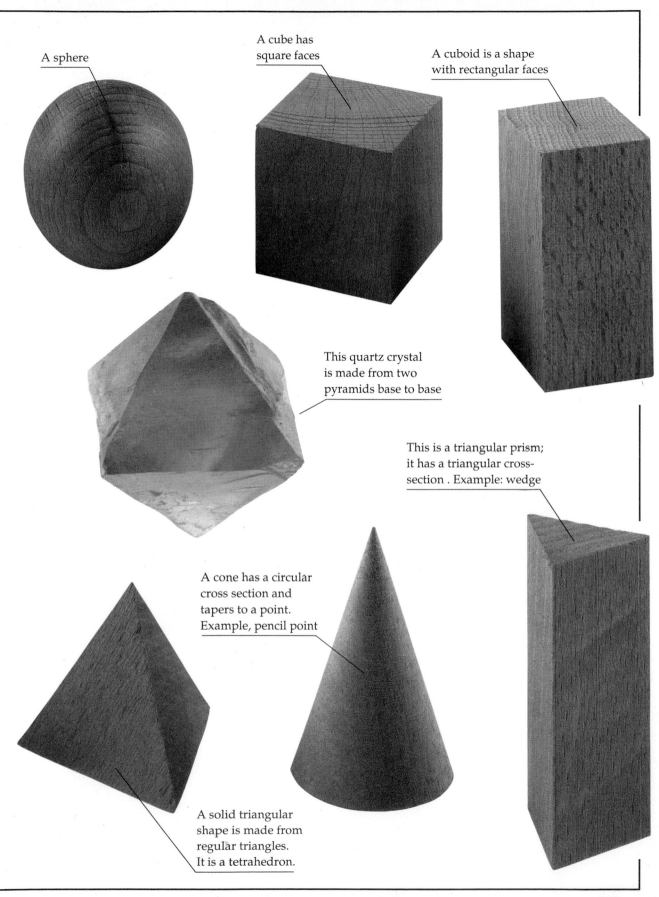

A sphere

A cube has
square faces

A cuboid is a shape
with rectangular faces

This quartz crystal
is made from two
pyramids base to base

This is a triangular prism;
it has a triangular cross-
section . Example: wedge

A cone has a circular
cross section and
tapers to a point.
Example, pencil point

A solid triangular
shape is made from
regular triangles.
It is a tetrahedron.

31

Making regular solids

Regular solids are those where every face is the same. For example, a cube is a regular solid based on square faces; a tetrahedron is a solid where all of the faces are triangles.

You can see clearly how solids are made from patterns of regular shapes by making them out of stiff paper. On the opposite page two patterns are given for you to copy.

Investigate solids
You can make any of the solids from patterns of flat shapes. When placed out this way they make a **net**. Ask a grown-up to make a larger photo-copy of the nets on these pages onto coloured paper. Cut round the edge of the net and fold along each of the edges. Put glue on the tabs and carefully stick the tabs and edges together.

Strange properties
Make a solid tetrahedron and paint each of the four faces with a different colour. While the paint is wet, roll the tetrahedron around on a piece of white paper. The colours will never intermingle no matter which way it is rolled.

This experiment will help you to discover why you only need four colours to show clearly all the countries in the world on a map.

The net for a tetrahedron

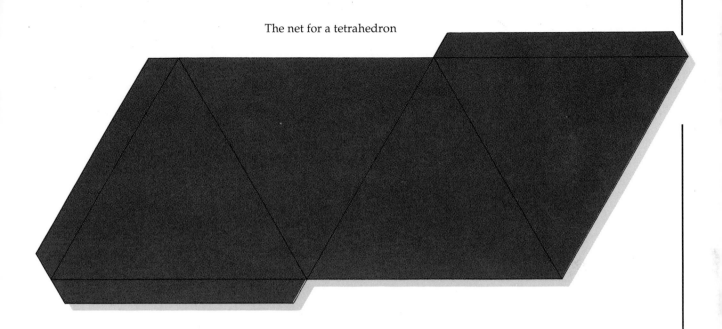

The net for an icosahedron

Tab

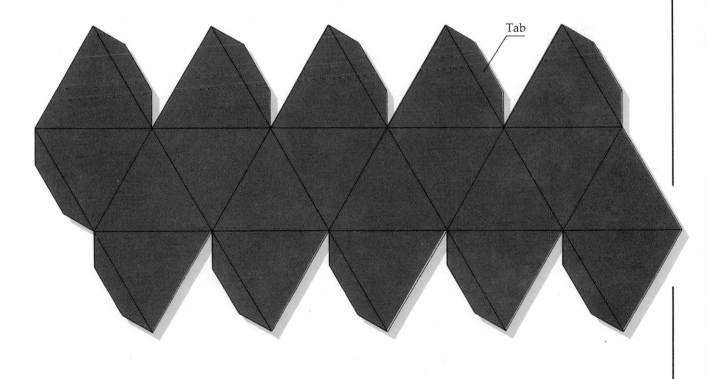

Symmetry

Many shapes are so regular when a line is drawn down the middle of it each half is exactly the same as the other. It is said to be a mirror image. This is one type of **symmetry**. Symmetries are fun to find; they are also important properties of shapes.

Place your mirror along this line

Simple symmetry
A shape can that can be folded onto itself has one plane of symmetry. You can check for symmetry by placing a mirror on the centre line of the picture on the right to see the full shape of each of these animals.

(For more information about using mirrors and symmetry, see the book Light *in the Science in our World series.)*

Turning symmetry
This is a sea urchin shell. It has five sets of plates all arranged symmetrically round an axis.

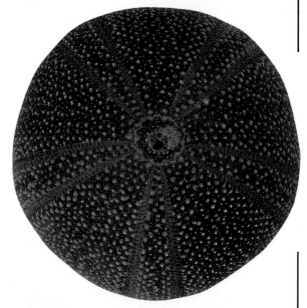

Turning symmetry
A plain ball can be spun on an axis and it will always look the same. This is called turning symmetry.

The marble in the picture above, however, has an irregular coloured pattern inside so that when the marble is spun the pattern always looks different. This marble has no symmetry!

How symmetrical are eggs?
This picture shows a wide range of egg shapes. How many types of symmetry do they seem to have at first glance?

Place a mirror on each egg in the picture until its reflection makes the egg whole again. This is the line of symmetry.

Now collect some eggs from a shop and find out if they have turning symmetry, that is, can you find a place where the eggs will spin and always appear the same?

Chemical patterns

Everything in the Universe is made from tiny particles called **atoms**. Atoms can hold together in patterns rather in the same way as if they could hold hands.

When atoms of all one kind 'hold hands' they make an **element.** For example, iron is made up only of iron atoms.

When two or more different types of atoms 'hold hands' they make a new substance with new properties called a **compound**.

A simple way to think about an atom is to imagine it as a ball. The sticks are like hands, linking atoms together. The model below shows an atom so small it cannot be seen even with the most powerful microscope. All the substances in the Universe are made from patterns using just 105 elements!!

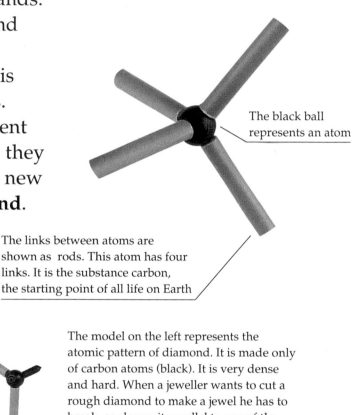

The black ball represents an atom

The links between atoms are shown as rods. This atom has four links. It is the substance carbon, the starting point of all life on Earth

The model on the left represents the atomic pattern of diamond. It is made only of carbon atoms (black). It is very dense and hard. When a jeweller wants to cut a rough diamond to make a jewel he has to break, or cleave, it parallel to one of the sides made by the atomic patterns

In this piece of Kimberlite rock, the yellow patches are diamond

What are molecules?

A **molecule** is the smallest possible number of linked atoms.

The compound water, for example, is made up of closely packed atoms of hydrogen and oxygen arranged in a regular way. The atoms always make six-sided shapes – hexagons.

Water can most easily be seen to be made from hexagons when it makes ice crystals (snowflakes).

A six-sided pattern can be seen in a snowflake. Each substance, whether it be snowflake or plastic is made of the same basic atomic pattern, explaining why a substance keeps the same properties no matter how large or small it is

This is a model of the arrangement of the atoms in water

Crystals

Crystals are the solid forms of substances, having a definite shape and a definite number of faces. Many form beautiful and amazing shapes. These shapes all fall into one of seven categories of shape known as crystal systems. All crystals of the same substance have the same basic shape, although they may differ in size.

Crystals

In special circumstances the pattern of atoms can become very ordered and form solid objects with flat sides. These are called crystals.

Crystals grow by adding to their surfaces, so a crystal can be artificially grown from a seed crystal.

It is easy to see why the crystals on this page are called cubic crystals when you compare them with this cube

Chlorine atoms

Sodium atoms

It is not always easy to see the individual crystals in a mineral. This piece of rock salt, for example, is a jumble of salt crystals and so it is said to be crystalline. Rock salt is mined to make table salt

Salt cubes

Pour a small amount of table salt onto a sheet of dark-coloured paper and look at it through a small hand lens. You should be able to see that each grain of salt is a small cube. Each one of these tiny crystals is made from the same arrangement of the molecules as shown in the diagram above.

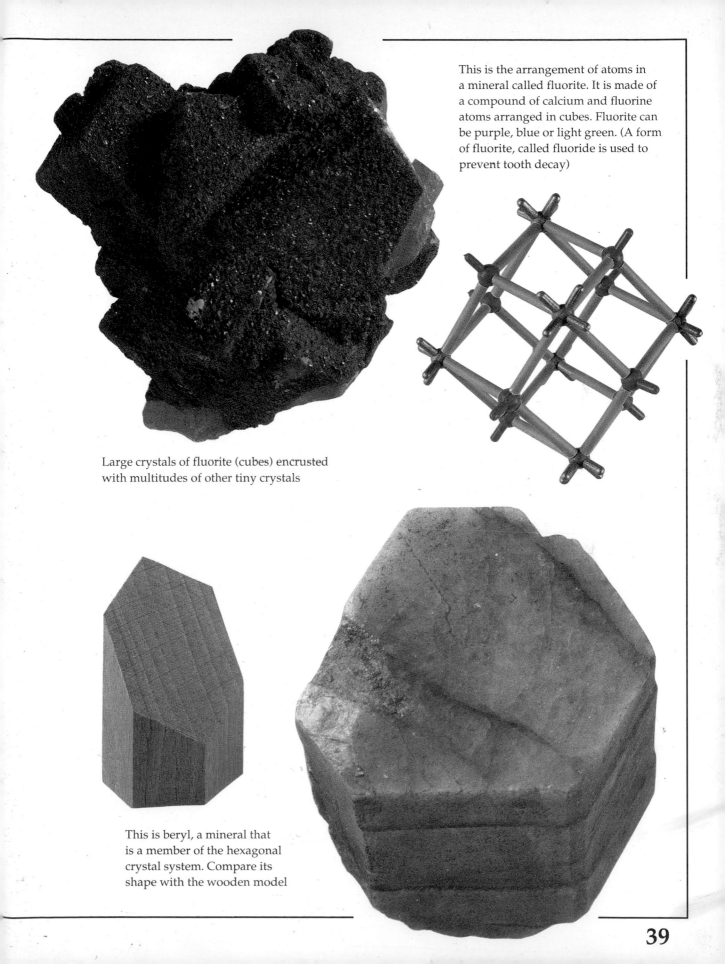

This is the arrangement of atoms in a mineral called fluorite. It is made of a compound of calcium and fluorine atoms arranged in cubes. Fluorite can be purple, blue or light green. (A form of fluorite, called fluoride is used to prevent tooth decay)

Large crystals of fluorite (cubes) encrusted with multitudes of other tiny crystals

This is beryl, a mineral that is a member of the hexagonal crystal system. Compare its shape with the wooden model

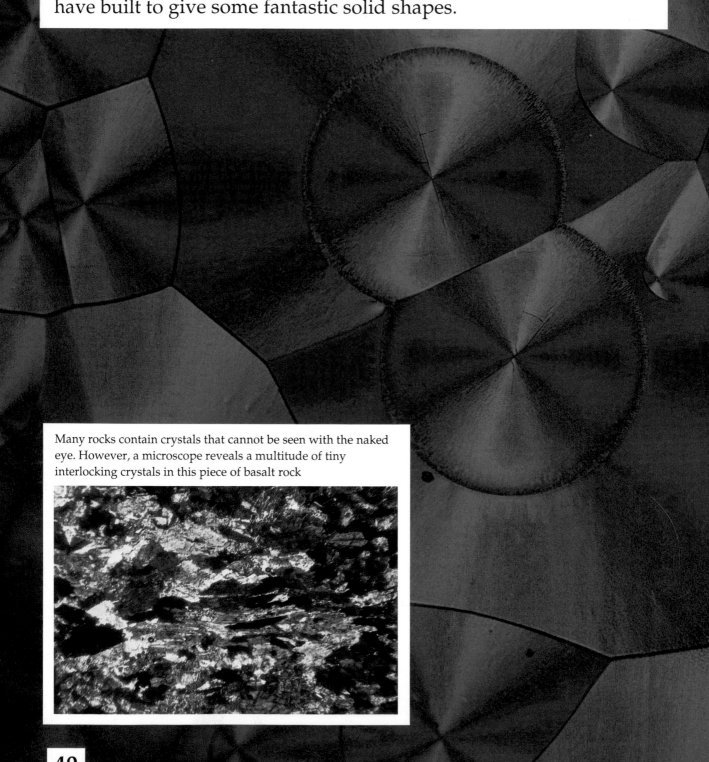

Crystals under the microscope

Many crystals are seen most clearly under the microscope. On this page you can easily see how atoms of some common substances have built to give some fantastic solid shapes.

Many rocks contain crystals that cannot be seen with the naked eye. However, a microscope reveals a multitude of tiny interlocking crystals in this piece of basalt rock

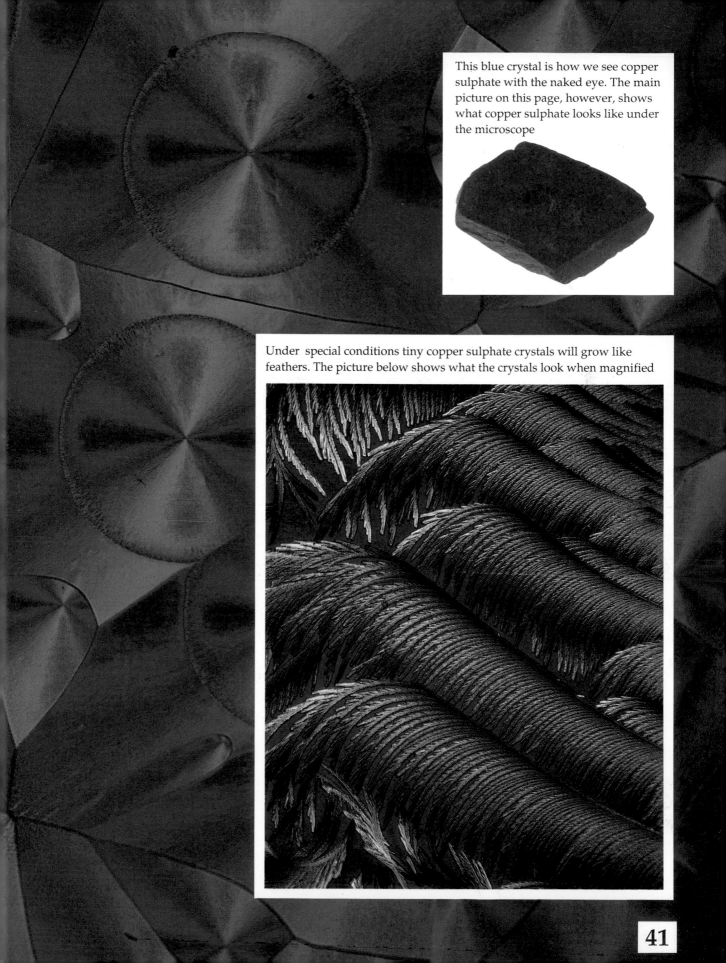

This blue crystal is how we see copper sulphate with the naked eye. The main picture on this page, however, shows what copper sulphate looks like under the microscope

Under special conditions tiny copper sulphate crystals will grow like feathers. The picture below shows what the crystals look when magnified

Making new materials

By rearranging the patterns made by atoms, chemists are able to produce new chemicals. Sometimes these can be of great benefit, as for example producing new medicines or an improved form of plastic. Here is an example of how oil is made into plastic.

Crude oil is a thick black liquid that is a mixture of many chemicals

These are the atoms we will use to see how new materials are made. The black ones are carbon and the white ones are hydrogen. These atoms are found in all living things. Notice how each of the atoms has a different number of links.

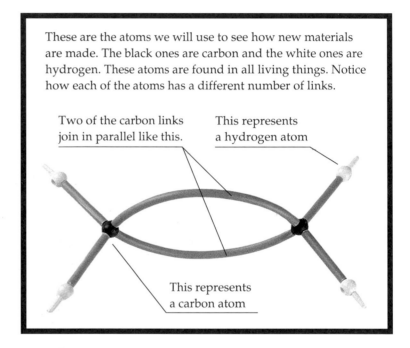

Two of the carbon links join in parallel like this.

This represents a hydrogen atom

This represents a carbon atom

1 When crude oil is heated in a refinery it releases many separate pure chemicals. One of these is a transparent gas called ethylene.

2 Ethylene is made of carbon and hydrogen atoms bonded together in the way shown above. To make a new material one of the carbon links must be 'unclipped'.

3 By heating ethylene one of the two carbon links can be made to 'unclip' and when this happens new forms of linking can occur.

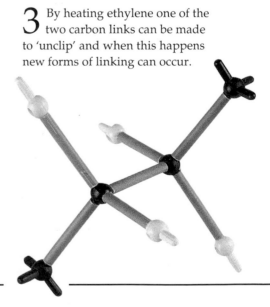

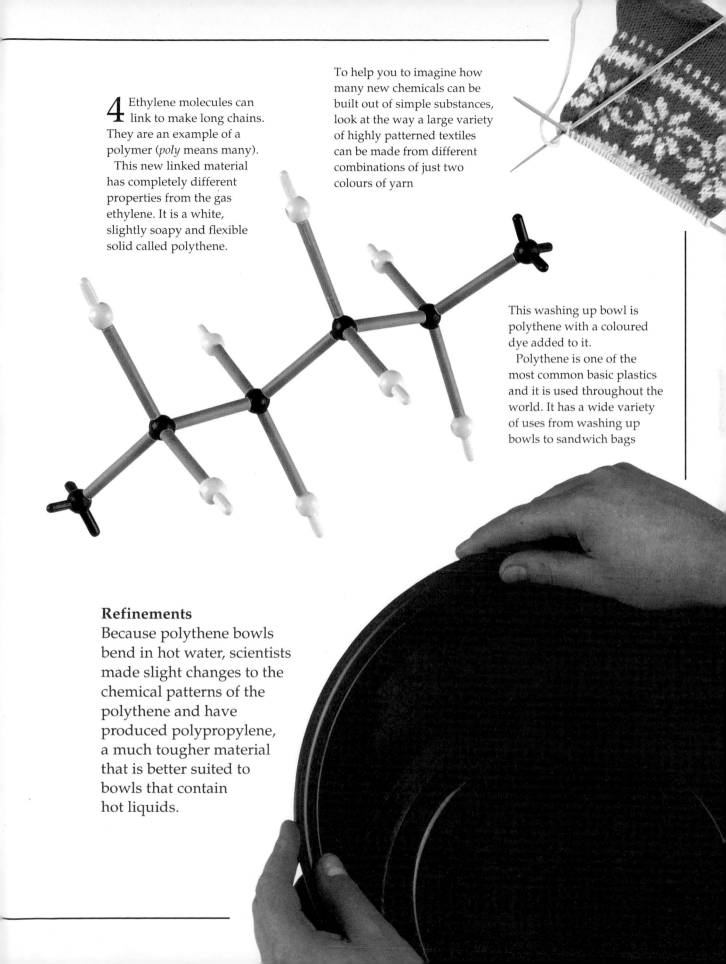

4 Ethylene molecules can link to make long chains. They are an example of a polymer (*poly* means many).

This new linked material has completely different properties from the gas ethylene. It is a white, slightly soapy and flexible solid called polythene.

To help you to imagine how many new chemicals can be built out of simple substances, look at the way a large variety of highly patterned textiles can be made from different combinations of just two colours of yarn

This washing up bowl is polythene with a coloured dye added to it.

Polythene is one of the most common basic plastics and it is used throughout the world. It has a wide variety of uses from washing up bowls to sandwich bags

Refinements

Because polythene bowls bend in hot water, scientists made slight changes to the chemical patterns of the polythene and have produced polypropylene, a much tougher material that is better suited to bowls that contain hot liquids.

Patterns in life

A living thing is the most complicated example of patterns and shapes. Every form of life begins as a single cell. By splitting and growing, and by cells changing and becoming more and more specialised, a single cell multiplies and eventually becomes an adult containing thousands of billions of cells.

Life's program

All the information for living things to be created is contained in a tiny piece of material – a form of living computer program – called DNA.

The DNA is a tiny, incredibly complex structure. It consists of two coils twisted together that lie in the **nucleus** of a cell. It contains all the instructions for forming all the cells in the body. Each piece of information is called a gene, and the DNA program is called the genetic code.

The cells of a plant stalk can be seen on the right in all their beauty. They are built from genetic information carried in each plant seed.

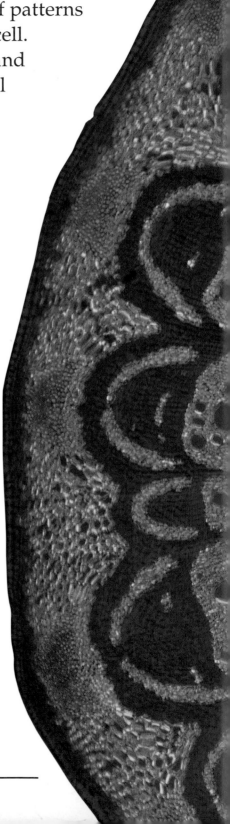

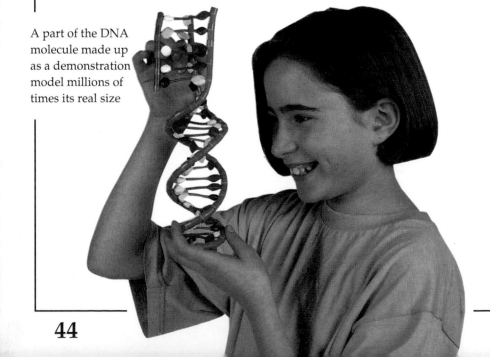

A part of the DNA molecule made up as a demonstration model millions of times its real size

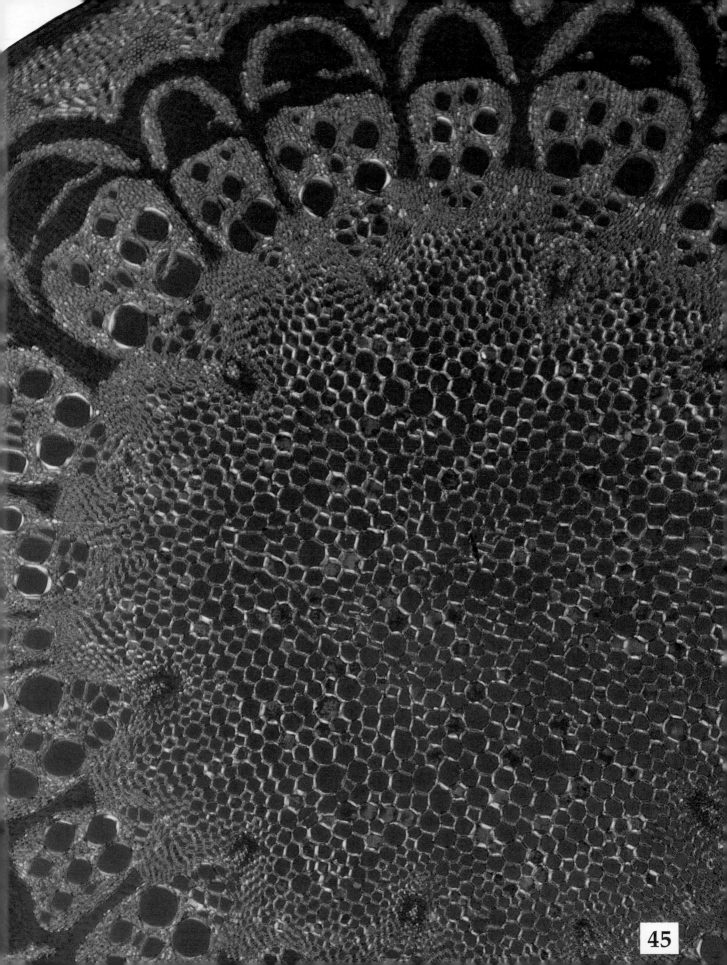

New words

atom

the smallest unit of an element.
It consists of a nucleus in which
there are protons and neutrons, and
a set of electrons which surround it.
Atoms are too small to be seen even
with the most powerful microscope

binary system

the system of numbers using only
zeros and ones. The system is most
useful for computers which rely
on yes-no instructions for all
their calculations

chaos

a form of disorder. People describe
something as chaotic when they
can recognise no pattern to it,
yet mathematicians have recently
begun to understand that what
seems without pattern may actually
be following some very simple rules

component

a small piece of a complex device
such as a computer. A component
will perform just one function, and
a designer uses many kinds of
component so that, when they are
put together, they can perform
many complex tasks

compound

a substance that it made from two
or more elements bonded together.
Water is a compound of the
elements oxygen and hydrogen

computer

a machine for processing information
at high speed. The principle of sending
simple commands was invented by
Henry Babbage in the 19th century, but
high speed computing became possible
only after the invention of the transistor
in the 1950s. Computers use patterns
of binary numbers as instructions

dimension

one of the basic measurements of the
Universe. The three dimensions are
length, mass and time

diode

a simple electronic device that can emit
a beam of light when an electric current
is passed through it

element

one of the 105 known basic substances
made from patterns of similar atoms.
Examples include gold and oxygen

formula

an expression which describes a rule
of some kind

laser

a device that produces a beam of very
intense light with very sharply defined
edges. The most common type of laser
beam is a red colour and comes from
a crystal of ruby

molecule

the smallest unit that can be recognised
as a compound, consisting of two or
more different atoms

net
the outline of a solid shape drawn onto
a sheet of paper

nucleus
part of the innermost region of a cell

parallelogram
a rectangular shape that has been
distorted so that both opposite pairs of
sides are still parallel to each other, but
the corners are no longer at right angles

prism
a shape with a constant cross section,
but which is long in comparison to
its section, rather like the shape you get
when toothpaste is squeezed from a
tube. The word prism is also used for
a piece of triangular glass used in
binoculars

random
events in time and space
which appear to have no
pattern to them. Random
events include the
numbers produced
by chance throws
of a pair of dice

symmetry
the way many objects
are arranged such that
they have parts which
are the same shape arranged
either side of a line or around
an axis. For example most bodies
are symmetrical about a line drawn
from the head to between the legs

tessellation
a mosaic or pattern built up of many
items all with the same shape and
which will fit together without
leaving any gaps. Triangles are
examples of shapes that tessellate,
whereas pentagons will not

tributary
a tributary is a channel that flows
into the main stem of a river system

unique
the only one of a particular type

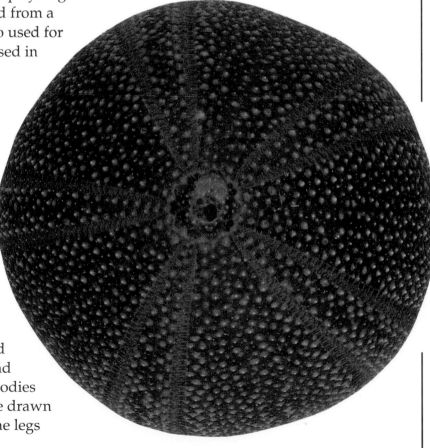

Index